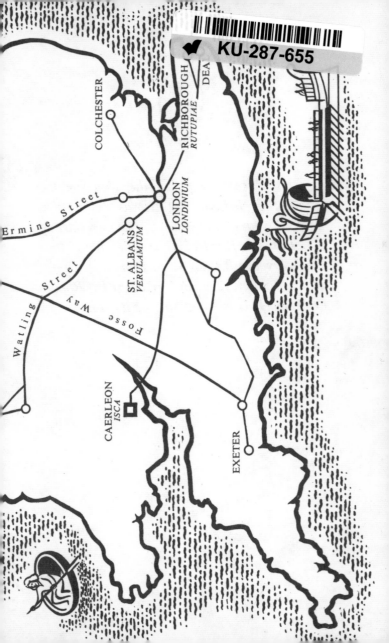

Series 561

Julius Caesar prepared the way for the conquest of Britain, but it was not until a hundred years later that it became part of the Roman Empire. For the next four hundred years Britain was a Roman Province, under Roman Law and guarded by Roman Legions. This is something of its story.

Helen
Francis

JULIUS CAESAR and ROMAN BRITAIN

by L. DU GARDE PEACH, O.B.E., M.A., Ph.D., D.Litt.

with illustrations by JOHN KENNEY

Publishers: Ladybird Books Ltd . Loughborough
© Ladybird Books Ltd (formerly Wills & Hepworth Ltd) 1959
Printed in England

JULIUS CAESAR
AND ROMAN BRITAIN

Long before the Romans conquered Britain, men had lived in these islands for hundreds of years. Some of them had come from northern countries like Norway or Denmark, others from France and Spain.

These people were divided into many tribes, each under its own chief. They lived in villages, in houses made of wattle and daub, that is, wooden poles and branches twisted together and covered with dried clay. These houses were usually just one room, thatched with reeds, and with a hole in the roof above the open fire. There was no glass in the small openings which let in the light, and they must have been very cold and draughty.

The men were mostly farmers, growing corn and grazing cattle. Their farming tools were made of bronze or iron by smiths, who also made swords and simple helmets; potters made bowls and jugs for domestic use.

The men and women wore brightly coloured clothes made of wool, and the wives and daughters of the chiefs had golden bracelets and necklaces, which may still be seen to-day in museums up and down the country.

4

7214 0166 X

Those of the Britons who lived by the sea were fishermen as well as farmers, and all of them fished in the rivers, which were cleaner than they are now.

The boats which the fishermen used were called coracles. They were very unlike the boats used to-day, although similar boats may still be seen in parts of Wales.

The coracles of the Britons were made of willow branches woven into what looked like a large shallow basket. This was covered on the outside with skins and then made waterproof with the resin or gum from pine and other trees. These little boats were very light, and the fisherman could easily carry his boat from his house to the lake or river.

Because they were round and flat, they were also very difficult to upset, and even on a rough sea they were safer than the rowing boats of to-day. On the West Coast of Ireland coracles are still used by the islanders of Great Blasquet to cross the rough waters of the Blasquet Sound, and wrecks are said to be quite unknown.

The people who lived in Britain had very little to do with the continent of Europe before the Romans conquered our island. The open sea between Britain and France was much wider than the Blasquet Sound, and only very daring sailors crossed it to sell things made in Britain, or to buy from the people of Gaul, the name by which France was then known.

Then, fifty-five years before the birth of Christ, the great Roman general, Julius Caesar, decided to bring his legions across the sea to Britain. It is doubtful whether he meant to make Britain a part of the Roman Empire: probably he only wanted to find out if it was worth conquering.

It was in August, in the year 55 B.C., that Caesar sailed to Britain with about 12,000 soldiers in eighty ships. They arrived off the coast near where Deal is now, but when the Roman soldiers saw the Britons waiting with spears and swords and chariots, ready to fight them as they landed, they refused to leave the ships.

Then the Standard Bearer of the X Legion leapt into the water and called on the soldiers to follow him. Fearful that the Standard might be captured by the Britons, the soldiers swarmed ashore and the Britons were beaten.

The Romans did not stay very long in Britain in 55 B.C., but in the following year Julius Caesar came again. This time he came in July, with many more soldiers, determined to conquer the island.

The Roman army landed in about the same place as before, and marched north-west towards where London stands to-day. The British attacked them in chariots and on foot, but the Romans had better arms and armour, and were much better trained. The Britons could do nothing to stop them.

Caesar and his men crossed the River Thames by a ford, somewhere above London, and continuing north-westwards reached the British stronghold or fort of the Catuvellauni. This was a very powerful tribe ruled by a chieftain called Cassivelaunus, who had made himself king of most of south-east Britain.

Caesar's soldiers captured the fort, and on the site of it built the town of *VERU-LAMIUM,* which to-day we call St. Albans.

Cassivelaunus submitted to Caesar, and gave him hostages. This means that Caesar took back with him to Rome some important Britons, who would be killed if Cassivelaunus revolted after the Romans had gone.

After the defeat of Cassivelaunus the Romans left Britain alone for a hundred years. The British rulers were supposed to pay tribute to Rome, but often it was not paid, and the Romans did not think it was worth while to send soldiers to collect it.

Then, in the year 43 A.D., the Roman Emperor Claudius sent a general called Aulus Plautius with 40,000 men to conquer Britain all over again. At first the Romans found it very difficult, but reinforcements, including some elephants, were brought by the Emperor, and in just over a fortnight the whole of the south of Britain had been subdued.

The Romans were very practical people, and the first thing they did in Britain was to make and fortify the ports where they landed their soldiers and supplies. From these ports the great Roman roads, many of them still in use to-day, went in long straight lines across country to London.

One of these ports was called by the Romans *RUTUPIAE,* the town which we to-day call Richborough. Here may be seen part of the Roman fortress, still standing, and the beginnings of the Roman road known as Watling Street, which goes right across England to Chester, called by the Romans *DEVA*.

Although the Romans were in occupation of Britain, there were many British men and women, hidden away in the great forests and swamps, who refused to submit. These men were fierce fighters, and they would steal out of their hiding places and attack small Roman forts or outposts. Then, when the Romans brought up reinforcements, they would again disappear into the forests where the Romans could not find them.

One of the bravest and most famous of these British warriors was called Caractacus. He gathered groups of men together wherever he could and as a Roman writer called Tacitus tells us, "by many a successful battle, raised himself far above all the other generals of Britain"

Gradually the Romans drove Caractacus and his men westwards into the mountains of Wales, and when he was beaten there in a battle near where Church Stretton, in Shropshire, stands to-day, he fled to Yorkshire, to the British tribe called the Brigantes.

But then the Queen of the Brigantes treacherously handed him over to the Romans, who were very glad to capture the leader of the British still fighting against the Roman Empire.

When the Romans won a war or conquered a new country, they held what was called a "Triumph". This was a procession through the streets of Rome, when everyone crowded the pavements to cheer the victorious general and his soldiers.

In addition to the soldiers, these triumphal processions included prisoners taken in the campaign, many of whom were afterwards either killed or sold as slaves. Large waggons were part of the show, piled high with all sorts of treasures captured from the enemy. The sound of the trumpets, the cheering of the crowds, and the tramp of the marching men, must have echoed round the Forum.

The central figure in the procession was always the victorious general. He rode in a richly decorated chariot, crowned with the laurel wreath of a conqueror. And always beside him he had a slave whose duty it was to whisper to him from time to time, "Remember, general, that you are mortal". This was so that the general should remain humble despite the cheering multitudes.

Caractacus was the chief prisoner in the "Triumph" which followed the conquest of Britain. As he marched in chains through the streets of Rome, he must have thought longingly of the distant homeland he was never to see again.

The Romans remained in Britain for three hundred and fifty years, and during that time they built many towns. Strangely enough, London was not the chief town in early Roman times. The capital city, from which the island was first governed, was St. Albans.

Many of these towns were large. The walls of St. Albans were two miles round, and the town covered 200 acres of land. The Roman name for St. Albans was *VERULAMIUM* or *VERULAM*, but we often know where Roman towns have stood from the names of the English towns which were later built on their ruins. Modern towns ending in -chester or -caster, like Dorchester or Lancaster, were once Roman, because these endings come from the Latin word *castra* meaning a camp or a fortified place.

The larger towns would have a theatre, open to the sky, with stone seats in a great semi-circle. Towns in which a legion of soldiers was quartered, like York or Caerleon, always had an amphitheatre, like the Coliseum at Rome, but on a smaller scale and built on banks of earth. Here all sorts of games were played and military exercises carried out by the soldiers.

The British tribes were not all willing to settle down quietly under Roman rule. Some were more warlike than others, and one of these was the tribe of the Iceni, who lived in what is now Norfolk. In those days this part of England was covered with swamps, and the Roman soldiers had never completely conquered it.

Less than twenty years after the Roman invasion, the men of the Iceni revolted under their warlike Queen, Boadicea. They had been very badly treated by the Roman soldiers and tax gatherers, and were determined to take a terrible revenge.

The Roman army was far away fighting in North Wales, when Boadicea, with many thousands of fighting men, destroyed first the Roman town of Colchester, and then, soon afterwards, the towns of London and St. Albans. These towns were all burned to the ground, and everyone in them massacred.

The Romans did what they could. A Roman legion was at Lincoln, and when news came to the commander of the revolt of the Iceni, he marched south with 2,000 Roman soldiers. But Boadicea had nearly 100,000 Britons under her command, and of the Romans, only the commander and a few horsemen escaped.

The Roman Governor of Britain at that time was a famous soldier named Suetonius. Although he was in the middle of a campaign against the men of Wales, he decided that he must march across England and attack Boadicea and the Iceni as soon as possible.

He had about 10,000 trained Roman soldiers with him, and although Boadicea had ten times that number, Suetonius had no doubt that the training and discipline of the Roman army would give him the victory.

So he marched towards London, having first ridden ahead with his cavalry in an attempt to save the city. When this failed, he rejoined his marching troops.

No one knows where the battle was fought, but Suetonius drew up his men on the slope of a hill, protected by woods on both sides. The British thought that the Romans were trapped and unable to get away, and they crowded in between the woods to attack them.

At the right moment, when Boadicea's men were too crowded together to use their arms, the Romans charged, and the British were decisively beaten.

On the top of the hill, watching the battle with Suetonius, was a young Roman officer named Agricola, who was afterwards to be the best Roman Governor Britain ever had.

At the time of the Roman conquest of Britain, the people who lived in these islands were not Christians. They worshipped many heathen gods in different parts of the country, and the gods of one district were often quite unknown outside the area of the tribe. These gods had names like Nodens, the god of hunting in the Forest of Dean, or Condatis, the god of the river Wear in Durham.

The religious leaders of the people were called Druids, and they were very powerful as well as learned. The Romans knew that they were using their power over the people to stir up rebellion against Rome, and decided that they must all be put to death. This was not easy because the Druids lived, and held their gatherings, in groves hidden away in the thick forests with which much of the country was covered.

Most of the Druids were in the Isle of Anglesey, off the coast of North Wales. So Suetonius decided to capture Anglesey, which the Romans called *MONA,* and put an end to the power of the Druids for ever.

To do this he had to cross the Menai Straits, his cavalry swimming their horses and his foot soldiers being ferried on rafts. Although the Druids fought furiously, all were destroyed.

The young officer, Agricola, knew that the only way to rule the people of Britain was to make friends with them.

So Agricola travelled widely in Britain, meeting all sorts of people from the various tribes, and talking to them. He always tried to find out what they thought and what they wanted, and when later on he himself became Governor of Britain, he knew far more about the British people than any other Roman.

It was not easy for the Romans to become friends with people whom they had only recently conquered, and many of whom had hoped that Boadicea would drive the Romans out of Britain. Agricola appreciated this, and his way was to go hunting with British guides and hunters in the big forests which largely covered the country.

These forests contained many wild animals, including bears and packs of savage wolves. As these were a danger to sheep and cattle, the Britons were glad to see them hunted and killed. It was probably over the camp fire, after a day's hunting, that Agricola really came to know and understand the British people.

Agricola remained about two years in Britain, performing his military duties as a young officer. He then returned to Rome, and after the Roman custom, spent the next ten years learning about the law and the way in which the Roman Empire was governed.

When he returned to Britain he was no longer a young officer, but an experienced soldier who knew all about the art of government. He was now to command the famous XX Legion, stationed at Chester, which the Romans called *DEVA*.

This was in the year 70 A.D., when the Romans had been nearly thirty years in Britain. Many Britons could not remember a time when the country had been free, and it seemed quite natural to them to be governed, not by British kings or chiefs, but by Governors sent from Rome.

There were still three legions of Roman soldiers in the country, but everything was now so quiet that the soldiers spent most of their time enjoying themselves in sports or at the games in the amphitheatres.

Agricola knew that there were still plenty of older Britons who hated the Roman rule, and the soldiers of the XX Legion soon learnt that their new commander would not allow them to become careless of their military duty.

Although Britain was now fairly peaceful, the Romans realised that at any moment some tribe might try to revolt. So they built forts in many parts of the country, in which they stationed small groups of soldiers.

It must have been very dull for the soldiers living in some little fort amongst the hills, far away from anywhere. Worse still, the Romans were used to the sunshine of Italy, and the long, cold, foggy winters of northern Britain must have made them very miserable.

Many of the Roman soldiers came from the south of Italy, or from the near East, and they were not used to snow and ice. We can imagine how they disliked being on sentry duty on the battlements of a Roman fort, with a snow blizzard blowing from the north-east.

Nor were they very much better off when they came off duty. The houses which the rich Romans built for themselves in the south of Britain had central heating, and even glass in the windows, but the little forts of the northern hills had neither. The wet, cold soldiers had nothing but charcoal fires round which to try to get warm.

It would be wrong to think of the Roman soldiers as doing nothing but man the garrison forts up and down the country. There was plenty of work to be done in Britain. For one thing, there were no proper roads when the Romans came.

If we look at a map of England to-day, we see that there are great main highways running across the country, often in long straight lines, from one town to another. There is, for instance, the road known as Watling Street, 259 miles long, which starts from the coast near Dover, and runs through London across the centre of England to Chester. This was one of the roads, still in use to-day, which was built by the Romans.

Wherever the Romans went, they built roads. As they conquered most of Western Europe, as well as North Africa and the near East, they needed roads along which the legions could march from one place to another. It was also along these roads that the trade of the Empire was carried.

Roman roads were built mostly by the soldiers of the legions, and were very well made indeed. The earth was rammed hard, and alternate layers of clay and stones were built up to a thickness of three or four feet. The road was then finished off with a top layer of flat stones or flints, and a ditch was dug along each side to drain off the water.

When Agricola returned to Britain for the third time, he came as the Roman Governor.

He would cross the sea from Gaul in a Roman galley. This was a ship fifty or sixty feet long, with a row of oars on each side. The oars were worked by slaves, who were often chained to the seats on which they sat. This ship also had one or two large sails, which were often dyed with bright colours and patterns.

When Agricola arrived in Britain, he would find a busy port, very different from the beach landing made by Aulus Plautius thirty-six years before.

This would probably be the port of *RUTUPIAE*, which we call Richborough, and of the building of which we have already seen a picture. Here Agricola would find a well-built quay alongside which his ship would berth. This quay would be piled with bales and barrels and all sorts of merchandise from all over the world. Slaves and Britons, Roman soldiers, and negroes from Africa, would be working the cargo, operating the cranes, and storing the goods in large warehouses built of stone with red tiled roofs.

It would be a busy scene with, in the middle of it, the brass armour and scarlet tunics of the soldiers drawn up to receive the new Governor.

Agricola became Governor of all Britain in the year 79 A.D. For the next seven years the country was governed as well as it has ever been, before or since.

Fortunately we know a great deal about Britain at the time of Agricola, because a man called Tacitus, who was married to Agricola's daughter, wrote a book about it. In this book he also tells us of the way in which Agricola governed the country. These are his words, translated from Latin, the language of the Romans, into English.

"Agricola suffered no public business to pass through the hands of his slaves. He was not influenced by private favour, but chose the best men as likely to prove the most faithful. He knew everything, but was content to let some things pass un- noticed. He could pardon small faults, and use severity to great ones. Yet he did not always punish offenders, and was frequently satisfied with penitence. By sup- pressing abuses in his first year as Governor, he made the people realise that under good laws it was better to live at peace with the Romans, rather than to rebel against them."

It is no wonder that Agricola was con- sidered the best Roman Governor that Britain ever had.

By the year 80 A.D. most of England, and the greater part of Wales, had been conquered and pacified by the Romans. There remained the wild tribes known as the Picts north of the river Tweed, in the mountainous country of Scotland.

Agricola might have been content to leave these tribes in peace, had they been equally content to leave Britain in peace. This was not so. Numbers of these wild Picts came from time to time, raiding southward. So Agricola determined to march against them with his whole army.

Starting from York, the Romans crossed the border and marched northward into Scotland. As they went they built forts, and left in them garrisons of men with enough provisions to last for two years. Then they marched on, meeting and beating the Picts as they went.

For four years the campaign continued. In the third year, Agricola's army was supported by the Roman fleet, which sailed up the coast, keeping in touch with the soldiers on shore.

There is no doubt that Agricola would have conquered all Scotland if the Roman Emperor, Domitian, had not become jealous of his victories, and recalled him to Rome.

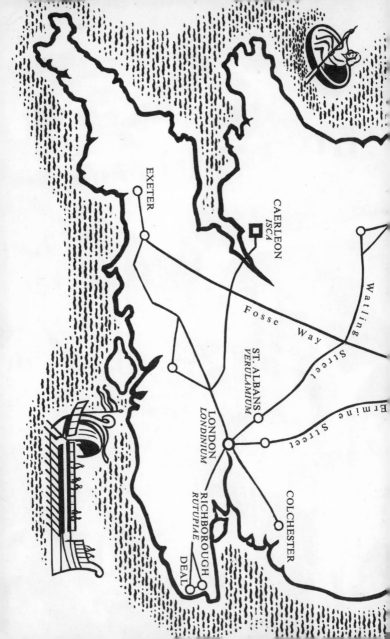

EXETER

CAERLEON
ISCA

Fosse Way

ST. ALBANS
VERULAMIUM

Watling Street

Ermine Street

LONDON
LONDINIUM

COLCHESTER

RICHBOROUGH
RUTUPIAE

DEAL

Roman towns in Britain were always built according to the same plan. Starting from the Forum, which often had a colonnade all round it, the rest of the streets in the town were set out like a chess board, all crossing one another at right angles. Along these streets were the houses in which the people lived.

The buildings in the Forum at Rome were all of white marble, and must have looked very dazzling in the Italian sunshine. Here in Britain very few buildings would be of marble. Mostly they would be of stone, plastered and painted, with roofs made of large red tiles.

The main streets were wide and well-made, with pavements and gutters, and in towns like London or St. Albans they would be crowded during all the hours of daylight. St. Albans was on the great highway of Watling Street, which ran through the middle of it. So in addition to the ordinary traffic of the town, the citizens would see soldiers of the XX Legion, starting out on their long march to join the Legion at Chester, or of the VI Legion on their way to York and Hadrian's Wall.

And they would go their ways contentedly and in peace, knowing that behind the sure shield of the Legions, Britain was safe.

The social centre of every Roman town of any size was the great building containing the baths. This usually occupied one side of the Forum, and contained, in addition to the hot and cold baths, the law courts, the municipal offices, school buildings and the gymnasium.

The Romans believed in keeping clean. They built wonderful baths, and used them two or three times a day. And always after the bath, the young Romans would go into the large high gymnasium to practise boxing and wrestling and all kinds of gymnastics.

At the same time, the Roman gymnasium was much more than merely a place for physical exercise. A great deal of business, the buying and selling of what we call stocks and shares, was done in it, and in many ways it served officially as a stock exchange.

There were places too, in this large building, where the Romans could buy food and drink. In fact, a Roman citizen could go to the baths in the morning and spend the whole busy day there, without wasting a moment.

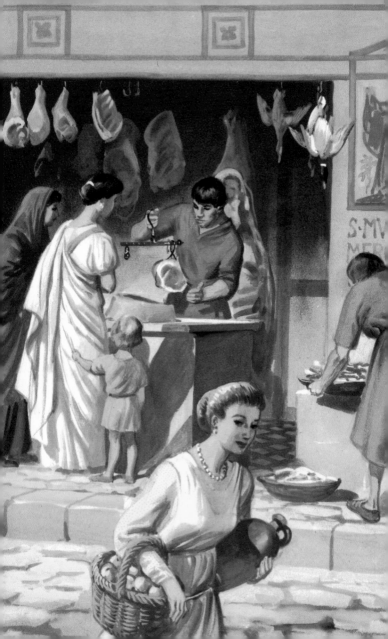

In peaceful Britain, south of the Wall, thousands of people lived their lives, just as they do to-day, going to school, or work, or doing the housework and the shopping.

The shops in a small Roman-British town were usually round two sides of the Forum, the large open space in the middle of the town where the main streets crossed. These shops had not got large plate-glass windows like shops to-day. They were, in fact, very simple, and exactly similar shops can still be seen in the back streets of Rome. They were simply houses with a big square opening in the front wall. Across this stretched a stone counter, behind which stood the shopkeeper. The customer stood in the street.

The shops were of all kinds. As well as the butchers, bakers and greengrocers, there were shoemakers and locksmiths, carpenters and jewellers. Tailors and leather workers could be seen at work behind their counters, and everywhere the merchants would be inviting the passers-by to purchase their goods.

The customers would be as varied as the merchants. Britons in rough woollen clothes, soldiers in scarlet and brass, women in graceful dresses and cloaks, men in togas, and slaves in short tunics everywhere. It was a busy scene.

During the time which the Roman occupation of Britain lasted, many hundreds of thousands of tons of merchandise and military supplies passed through the ports which linked these islands with the Continent.

The busy ports of Britain were well-built, with stone quays and warehouses. There were big cranes, worked by hand, to lift the cargo from the ships' holds, and there would be rows of carts ready to transport the merchandise along the good Roman roads to the customers.

The ships would seem small to-day. They were, of course, sailing ships, with banks of oars to help them along when the wind was light. The sails were dyed with bright patterns and the hulls of the ships themselves were painted and gilded. The high prows and sterns, carved and coloured, stood up bravely against the stone quay as the ships were unloaded.

The crews would be of all colours and languages. Arabs and negroes, Greeks and Phœnicians, Spaniards, Carthaginians, and Romans; they would come from anywhere between London and Constantinople. A Roman port in Britain was as noisy as it was colourful, as busy as it was international.

Thirty-six years after Agricola left Britain, another great Roman, the Emperor Hadrian, came to these islands. Hadrian was a great traveller and wherever he went in the Roman Empire he strengthened its frontiers.

Three years before there had been a serious rebellion in the North of Britain. The Caledonians and the Brigantes, the two great tribes north and south of the Scottish border, had risen in revolt and slaughtered the whole of the officers and men of the IX Legion, stationed at York.

The rebellion was crushed, but Hadrian decided that in future it should be made very much more difficult for the Picts to cross the border into peaceful Britain. So he set three legions of Roman soldiers, the II, VI and XX, about 20,000 men, the task of building a great frontier wall which ran right across the country from Newcastle to Carlisle, and long stretches of which can still be seen. In seven years it was finished.

Hadrian's Wall was seventy-three miles long, seven to ten feet thick, and eighteen to twenty feet high. It was built of stone, and it joined up a row of forts about five miles apart. There was a solid tower to hold 100 men every mile, and at every third of a mile a signal turret. It was the strongest of all the Roman frontier fortifications.

Agricola left Britain in the year 85 A.D., never to return. For the next three hundred and twenty-five years Britain remained a Roman province, governed by Roman Governors and protected by the Roman Legions. During this time there were long periods of peace, and Britain became a civilised country of roads and towns and villages.

The South of England was covered with the villas of wealthy Romans and Britons. These were large farmhouses, often with water laid on through pipes to elaborate baths. In the wilder north, the villas were less frequent, and the towns were well fortified to protect them from the tribes beyond the river Tweed. Now that Agricola had gone, these Picts were again raiding the peaceful lands to the south.

The Picts did not always come to raid the Roman settlements. Often they came to trade, and the hunting dogs and the sturdy ponies bred in Scotland were eagerly bought by the Romans. There would be very busy scenes outside the walls of some Roman fort when the Picts arrived with their fierce dogs, looking themselves almost as fierce and shaggy in their clothes of skins, and with wild, untamed hair and beards.